ANN SACKS

TILE
&
STONE

ANN SACKS

TILE & STONE

ANN SACKS

with Linda Leigh Paul

Rizzoli
NEW YORK

First published in the
United States of America in 1998 by
Rizzoli International Publications, Inc.
300 Park Avenue South,
New York, NY 10010

ISBN 0-8478-2159-5
LC 98-67161

Ann Sacks Tile & Stone
was prepared and produced by
Michael Friedman Publishing Group, Inc.
15 West 26th Street
New York, NY 10010

Editors: Francine Hornberger and
Reka Simonsen
Art Director: Jeff Batzli
Designer: Lori Thorn
Photography Editor: Sarah Storey
Production Manager: Camille Lee

Color separations by
Colourscan Overseas Co Pte Ltd.
Printed in Singapore by
KHL Printing Co Pte Ltd.

Acknowledgments

This book is dedicated to my husband Robert
and children David and Amy. To the talented and
generous tile artists, designers, and photographers
who have contributed to the book I want to express
my admiration and appreciation.

CONTENTS

INTRODUCTION

Tile and stone have been the building blocks of cultures and civilizations from ancient times to the present. Masterworks of art in architecture and construction have survived the wear and tear of the years and still retain their beauty and integrity. In all their manifestations, from paved walkways and mosaics to temples, pools, and fountains, tile and stone provide a unique opportunity to transform the purely functional into the beautiful and connect the past, the present, and the future.

The first paved walkway described in Athens was in the gardens at the Academy (341–271 B.C.). Little is known about it except that it was near the residence of Plato, whose neighbor Theophrastus maintained "a garden with a walk" (Christopher Thacker, *A History of Gardens*).

Ancient walkways, colonnades, and arcades were paved with tightly fitted pieces of marble or granite. Others were made with irregular, loose-fitting patterns. The stone used was particularly important in these settings. Designers relied on the

Opposite: The courtyard of the Villa Oplontis in Italy is a striking example of the beauty of stone. *Above:* Monumental columns gracefully define an ancient stone walkway in St. Peter's Basilica, Rome.

Above: The rugged stone used for these stairs in Rome has only grown more handsome with time and use. *Right*: These magnificent stone ruins have stood the test of time. They date back to ancient Rome's occupation of Carthage, during the first few centuries of the first millennium A.D.

stone's ability to absorb and radiate "heat by reflection…so it is pleasant in winter but still more so in summer when the terrace is kept cool in the morning" (*ibid*.). From the most sophisticated projects led by engineers and architects to the simple additions of terraces, decks, pools, sunrooms, and even master baths, the proper relationships of tile and stone to the environment can provide comfort, utility, and beauty far beyond any other materials.

Early gardens, pools, fountains, steps, stairways, terraces, courtyards, bridges, archways, and colonnades were all made of stone. The first stone "countertops" appeared in gardens in the form of outdoor dining tables featuring rotating marble surfaces, while nearby sat hand-carved, matching marble chairs for relaxation. Many of these once-outdoor amenities have moved into our homes today.

History records actual tiling as early as 3000 B.C. in Egypt. Although their ceramic achievements are comparatively uncelebrated because their first love was glassmaking, the Egyptians remain the first recorded tilers. They invented coated, multicolored mud bricks, that is, glazed tiles. Egyptian ceramic art consisted primarily of relief tiles presenting a distinct view of human forms, mythological beasts, and domestic animals. Ceramic bas-reliefs also recorded cultural symbols and, of course, the ancient Egyptians' belief in their preeminence among humans.

As evidenced by this culture, the history of tile as an art form is very rich and deep. Tile has always communicated many things about the earth and its people as well as the technology of certain times and places.

The Portuguese city of Conimbriga is known for its stunning floor mosaics, which date back to Rome's invasion in 139 B.C.

Ancient Persia later became the center of tiling techniques, which were to become refined in tile centers worldwide. In Persia, tile making was not an indigenous craft; the customs of the rulers, resources, and craftsmen were brought together from all over the known world. Collaborations resulted in tiles unique in form, color, and design. As characteristics from different areas emerged in the local ceramic work, what came to be called the "new eclecticism" developed, and it was for this style that the workmanship of the entire region became known as early as 500 B.C.

In Muslim countries, wealth and power were illustrated by the extent and richness of interior and exterior mosaic tiling, tile flooring, and other decorative tile elements. Mosaics in Muslim cultures were bright or even metallic, which reflected their art and climate. Mosaics in other cultures featured neutral-colored stones telling stories in somber tones. Mosaic is one graphic example of how tile can tell stories of cultures through the ages—both histories and myths have been depicted in mosaic.

A social pattern also emerged during ancient times, as independent craftsmen and potters migrated from one place to another and set up wherever there were workshops with kilns. These workshops attracted artisans from all regions who hoped to receive commissions for work. These congregations of potters evolved into tiling centers. Expert potters were even abducted and carried off by conquering rulers. This has made it difficult to identify the styles and traditions of specific locations. It is astonishing to see how craftsmen and their art endured centuries of exploitation and oppression, and the many ways in which tile making continued and

Ceramics as well as stone have a glorious ancient tradition. Muslim countries are known for vibrant, highly decorated tiles such as these—the ones on the left are from Iran; the ones on the right from Turkey.

Above: Jerusalem's beautiful mosque, the Dome of the Rock, was completed in 691. The architecture incorporates both stone and colorful tiles to wonderful effect. *Right*: A detail of the Dome shows the intricate designs painted on each tile, and the elaborate patterns that the combined tiles create.

even flourished during periods of overwhelming uncertainty and social disorder.

Many textiles, with the exception of some very beautiful carpets, have perished, but tiles remain. That is why selecting tile for your home is both exciting and challenging. You are choosing from a tradition as

enduring and varied as any in the art world. These aesthetic choices are all excellent enough to have withstood the test of time, and the material itself will surely outlast your home. Be consoled by the fact that there are few wrong choices to be made with these products if you work with a professional who can guide you to the classics, both ancient and modern.

In selecting tile today you may choose one of those periods to re-create in your home. Whatever you choose, tile and stone will be the permanent part of your home that expresses a great deal about art, culture, and design.

Opposite: The magnificent interior of the Dome of the Rock in Jerusalem, Israel. The rock in the center of the mosque marks the spot, according to Jewish tradition, where God prevented Abraham from sacrificing his son, Isaac. *Above*: A gorgeous floral ceramic tile design from Istanbul, Turkey.

This book is about creating a feeling in your home. As our lives change, so, too, do the practical requirements of choosing the objects we live with. Being happy with those choices usually means creating a balance between the things you love and the things that are necessary.

Throughout this book, I will help you discover not only how you want your home to look, but also how you want it to feel. Many families appreciate the warmth and serenity of a Tuscan villa but do not know how easily achievable characteristics of this style are through the use of tile and stone. At every turn we will look at the small steps to these more modest goals as well as to the ambitious projects unaffected by budget or time constraints.

Since tile and stone reflect the cultures in which they were first created, your selection of tile will often bring elements of that culture into your home. Understanding the culture from which your tile comes will often help you to connect the design to the feeling you wish to achieve. Precise tiles impart a very different feeling than those that are handcrafted. The generous use of color creates a different mood than creamy, light, neutral limestone, which serves as a background rather than a focus. While terra-cotta is used in many of the same cultures as limestone, the selection of one of these materials rather than the other sets a different tone for a home. In broad terms, terra-cotta is richer in color and texture and is more often the background for a comfortable, warm, even rustic interior. Limestone is more typically chosen for a more formal environment and one that is neutral in color. Making the selection between terra-cotta and limestone or, even more importantly, selecting tile or

Above: The simple, natural beauty of southern France can be brought into any home. Here, the sink and mirror are surrounded with cream-colored tiles that are decorated with understated relief designs. *Opposite:* The floor-to-ceiling design of this kitchen focuses on antiqued stone tiles in a broad range of natural hues—ocher, rose, and cream—above the grilling area. These colors echo the tones in the copper hood and stainless grill cover.

stone instead of wood is perhaps the most crucial decision that you will make about how you live in your home and how it looks and feels.

While traveling in France I found a lovely small-production tile factory in which a mother, father, and daughter kept the family tradition of tile making alive by producing hand-cut, brilliantly hand-glazed tile. I was drawn to their work and could not take my eyes from the pieces; the imperfections seemed "just so" and variations in the glazing were earthy and charming. But the tile strongly conveyed a sense of both rustic and urban French interior design, and was clearly inspired by the casual lifestyle and agrarian mind-set of the south. Such gifts had been borrowed for centuries by urban designers to soften the interiors of Paris and create peace within a city home.

I remember discovering a simple house in Hyères, France. Its flooring was simple, nineteenth-century terra-cotta. The golden and traditional red tones of the tile gave the house its character and made it memorable. You may have had a similar experience, and when you returned home, you looked at your own house and thought that all it would need was a terra-cotta and limestone floor in the kitchen, or perhaps a narrow terra-cotta pathway leading to the greenhouse and garden to capture that special feeling. Part three of this book will show you how these materials have been

(continued on page 20)

Opposite: Soft, warm-hued stone covers the floors and walls of this shower, and tile graces the ceiling and archway, providing protection from moisture in all directions. *Above*: The dark green of this kitchen's cabinetry is softened and warmed by the terra-cotta tiles used for the counter and backsplash. The earthy tones of antique terra-cotta floor pavers add to the feeling of being in a country home.

successfully reclaimed to be used in renovations and even new homes to give them the authentic character of Europe.

I hope you will enjoy perusing the pages of this book and that it will inspire you to use these lovely materials in designing your home. A great deal of thought goes into the selection of our varied collection. I always ask myself, "For whom is this tile or stone?" My appreciation is not limited to our products or our customers. I do not include only things

Above: Colorful and lustrous metallic-glazed tile adds a bold character to this small space. With this contemporary glazing technique, no two tiles are exactly alike. ***Opposite:*** High-gloss, brightly glazed tiles in a precise diamond pattern add crispness and vitality to the solid colors of the countertop and tub surround.

that are very expensive or rare, but believe every budget and most individual styles have been considered. I strive to continually expand the collection in each price and style category. There are lovely choices for everyone, from the discriminating urban dweller to the young couple renovating their first bungalow, from those who are conservative to those who want to express their youthful artistic style through tile. This is not a great challenge; I myself love each of these different styles for different reasons and in different ways. I am thrilled by simple rustic glazed tiles from Provence and equally enthu-

siastic about our exciting hammered metal and glass tiles. These could all be easily found together under one roof, as they are in my own house.

If you have the opportunity to visit an Ann Sacks showroom, you will see that creative ideas and individual attention to each home is what we are all about. New products constantly fuel ideas and drive the enthusiasm of our salespeople. Everyone is committed to changing the customers' response from overwhelmed to focused and excited. It is our passion for both tile and people that creates beautiful projects!

—Ann Sacks

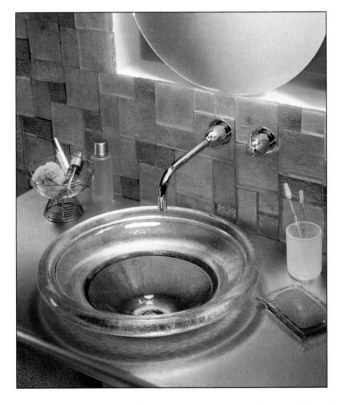

Opposite: Turquoise tiles add a bright splash of color to this streamlined modern shower.
Above, left: Translucent glass tile with a worn, hand-crafted feel gives an illusion of depth and openness to this backsplash. *Above, right*: Jewels of hand-crafted, fused art glass tiles, with their transparency and deliciously sweet colors, can transform any surface.

HUNDERTWASSER HOUSE/
FRIEDENSREICH HUNDERTWASSER (B. 1928)

Vienna-born Friedensreich Hundertwasser is an artist who has railed against the rigidities and conformities of classical and modern design for decades. A painter and an architect, he uses elements from nature as his motifs. His apartment building, completed in Vienna in the mid-1980s, is a comfortable habitat for residents that includes flowers in pots on windowsills and trees planted on balconies, terraces, and in alcoves.

Hundertwasser shows the influence that forms and color have in our daily lives. His vision is one in which design rejects tradition and uniformity to enable people to live more intimately with their surroundings. His desire for an environment that reflects feeling and passion led him to create an asymmetrical design, in accord with the lines of nature. The building actually curves; each window is unique; walls and floors undulate; and lines, where they occur, are all slightly askew.

The sensation one feels when entering the building is of the dynamic exuberance that was felt by the tile setters, bricklayers, and stone masons as they began to realize that they, too, had been set free to create their own personal visions. Hundertwasser's guidance ensured that their work would be judged not against an ideal—a perfectly straight line, for example—but rather as an individual expression of their craftsmanship. The results are stunning.

Hundertwasser's interiors are remarkable also in their innovative uses of tile. The flooring is sprinkled with uneven lines crossing the halls at intermittent points; they turn and run up the edge of a wall for several inches to burst into a bulb of mosaic colors. Lines made out of narrow triangular or rectangular pieces of tile that are laid end to end zip around the doorway and past the stairwell and disappear. The main entry is a sea of undulating, highly polished terra-cotta offset by random sections of colored tiles that look like light reflected from a nearby window.

Optical illusion is important to Hundertwasser's creations. In this case, rather than convincing the eye to see a rational and perfect world, the illusions create shifting, almost moving sensations with tile patterns that he believes provide a much needed relief from a too-rational world. A glossy white tile is installed against a white wall in a pattern that looks as if it is sliding toward the floor. The use of white does make an oblique reference to the traditional white marble and tile of baths and kitchens, but as our eye moves along the irregular lines of the pattern, we are invigorated by the contemporary references and possibilities.

The message of Hundertwasser is one that we try to convey in our showrooms: good design does not mean never personalizing or taking risks; it means looking to history for inspiration and then putting your personal stamp on a classic.

Hundertwasser's apartment building in Vienna has an affinity with Gaudí's Casa Battló in Barcelona.

PART ONE

TILE

Thousands of years of tile making have captured every historical moment in design, color, and form. Tile has been used to enhance temples, minarets, and cathedral spires that reach toward the sky, as well as tombs that delve under the earth. Archaeological evidence shows that tile making probably occurred in every culture and every climate because all that is needed to make a tile is clay, a source of water, and sun or fire for hardening.

Tile was used architecturally long before it was used for decoration. Tiles made up the first plumbing systems. The Romans heated their baths by running hot water through curved terra-cotta tiles (piping) under the marble floors of great buildings. Curved surface tiles were used for roofing to keep rainwater in a guided path. And of course, tile was used for

Opposite: The caldarium, or hot-water room, of the baths in the exquisite Alhambra Palace in Granada, Spain. *Above:* These geometric tiles in a convent cloister in central Portugal date back to the sixteenth century.

Top: Muslim tradition forbids the representation of living creatures in religious art, which is why the tiles in mosques such as the Rustem Pasa Cami Mosque in Istanbul, Turkey, bear intricate floral and geometric motifs. *Above:* An ornamental tiled panel at the Plaza d'Espania in Seville, Spain, shows the surrender of the Moors to the Christians, which occurred in 1248.

footpaths, walkways, flooring, and walls. Colors, glazes, molds, and firing techniques helped create sophisticated clay lattice tiles and terra-cotta pavers. Latticed window tiles manipulated the play of light and shade so effectively that shadows caused by the latticework appeared extremely dark and gave relief to eyes accustomed to glaring sunlight.

The British used the technique of deep inlay, which is highly durable, but the first flooring tiles came from Spain and Portugal during the second half of the twelfth century. British tile mosaics were small and square, made of hand-shaped clay rather than of random clay or stone fragments. And British mosaic flooring reached a superior quality in workmanship and detail, with curves, angles, squares, baguettes, triangles, and especially the lozenge creating trompe l'oeil images. Tile helps us to gain an appreciation of something very refined in design being created from very simple materials. That what most often remains intact in historic buildings is the tile reveals the astonishing durability of such simple materials and processes.

Tile making is also, at times, a means of story-telling. The stories are tales of countries and their rulers, daily life, fashion, power, and sometimes defeat. Murals and mosaics made from tiles depict romantic scenes, mythological gardens, hunting parties, the gods at play, and royal and pastoral lifestyles.

More often, however, patterns created with tile are geometrical rather than representational in design. Repeated shapes—much like a quilt—are the building blocks of most tile floors.

Above: Tiles decorated with stylized Arabic lettering and complex geometric designs contrast beautifully with rough stone in the Rustem Pasa Cami Mosque. *Left:* These basketweave-patterned ceramic tiles are from the Alcázar Palace in Seville. Made in the fourteenth century, they are imitations of the tiles at the Alhambra Palace in Granada.

A Sampling of Popular Tiles Available Today

TERRA-COTTA TILE

Simplicity and timeless beauty are the defining qualities of unglazed terra-cotta tile. Worldwide imports of terra-cotta give us a perspective on the kind of flooring that has been and is still used all over the world. Differences in these tiles are the result of variations in soil composition and firing techniques. The most important thing we can learn from these wonderful imports is that they represent centuries of uses in all sorts of households, from grand châteaus and villas to the farmhouses of the countryside.

The one characteristic common to all terra-cotta is warmth. That is not to say it is rustic, because in fact an old worn terra-cotta floor can be the ideal backdrop for formal antiques and is equally effective warming an interior of crisp, modern furnishings. Imagine black leather sofas softened by a charming terra-cotta floor. These tiles can be used in imaginative ways because they will never let you down. They only add to whatever you do—in their simplicity and strength they can play center stage or background equally well.

Our terra-cotta tiles are from France, Spain, Italy, Bali, Mexico, and America. They are found on

Opposite and above: This church office, transformed into a master bath, was designed by Cynthia Retzlaff Interiors. Antique blonde terra-cotta flooring and wall tiles blend perfectly with tumbled giallo (yellow) marble borders and the hand-formed white tile trim.

floors and walls, on patios, in pool areas, and in gardens all over the world extending far beyond their country of origin. Terra-cotta is the great foundation for relaxation and casual elegance in almost every culture. As a design choice, its many advantages include size, shape, color variation, texture, and superb livability. A brief explanation of types of terra-cotta may help you choose your own.

Today's terra-cotta from the famous studio in the Salernes region of France is available in handcrafted, traditional flooring sizes that show color variations from buckskin and wheat to deeper browns and reds. The magnificence of this tile is the result of nine days of wood firing, done in the same wood-fired kilns and in

Below, left to right: Classic southern French terra-cotta octagon tiles have a small floral insert in the center, while the traditional blonde terra-cotta octagon tiles have a matching insert. Traditional designs such as fleur-de-lis, crests, and stylized lions are still reproduced in terra-cotta.

the same manner as has been the tradition in Provence for centuries. This terra-cotta is not rustic, though it is completely handcrafted; it is refined without being perfect and is a superb choice for all interiors.

Just next door to this atelier in Salernes is the Provençal factory where jewel-like glazed tile is made. In fact, the two factories have for generations shared a cooperative clay quarry in their village.

This glazed terra-cotta from the south of France has all the beauty and imperfection of the unglazed pieces. The handsome watercolor effect of the hand-glazing and shading allows the terra-cotta body to make itself known to the viewer and is very dramatic. Through the beautiful glaze you can see clearly that each tile is unique.

Also available from France are machine-made terra-cotta tiles. A variety we are fond of is a very warm terra-cotta with ocher and russet shading. The machine-cut edges allow for precision installations, which can be easily cut and fitted with limestone borders. The overall appearance created is a light,

warm, subtly shaded floor—a perfect example of warm and contemporary style.

Today in Valencia, Spain, a family of artists is producing a dramatic, very rich terra-cotta called Torquemada, which has distinctive black flame marks from open-pit firing. The firing is fed by wood and olive pits and results in spectacular color variations from pale blonde to rich cordovan. The tiles each appear to have been passed through a veil of smoke. Flooring tiles are large—8" by 8" (20 by 20cm) or 10" by 10" (25 by 25cm)—and are rugged and irregular in appearance. The smaller squares are often used in concert with turquoise or white accent pieces or with lovely, tiny diamond-shaped border patterns.

Another beautiful Spanish terra-cotta is Tierra Valenciana, also from Valencia. On my first visit to this factory I looked out the window onto a remote road and noticed that the earth changed from brilliant ocher to lush salmon and terra-cotta just like

Left: Made of Spanish terra-cotta, these Tierra Valenciana field tiles are multihued, handcrafted, and wood-fired. *Middle*: Distinctive black smoke and flame colors the dark, rich Spanish "torched" field and diamond border tiles. Accent tiles are glazed in white. *Right*: This antique blonde terra-cotta is inset with triangles of deep cordovan terra-cotta to create an elegant, timeless design.

the tiles! It was an exciting and emotional experience to realize in a new way just why terra-cotta has been loved everywhere throughout time. It is the earth, practically unchanged.

Antique terra-cottas are a special product prized by us and our customers across America. Our collection is extensive and ever-changing, and no two customers ever receive the same floor. All antique tiles are certified by the customs authorities of their country of origin to be more than 150 years old. One can be assured that they are authentic because antiques are

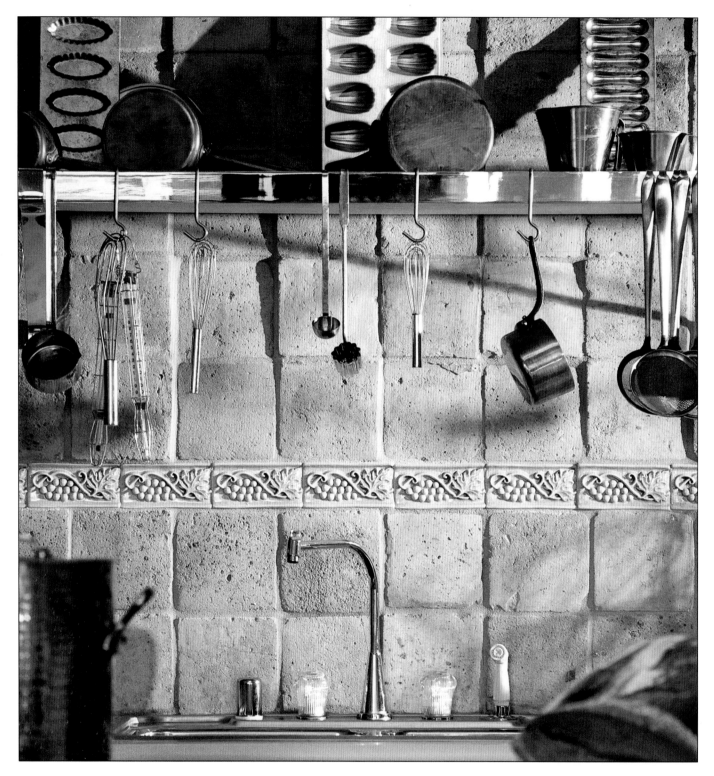

The texture of blonde French antique terra-cotta is accentuated in morning sunlight,
as are the irregularities in thickness. In this kitchen, a wall of field tile embellished with
a grapevine border creates a rustic, homey feeling.

duty-free; in approving these tiles as antiquities, the government agrees to give up the twenty-one percent duty that they collect for exporting tiles.

Customers always ask how such materials are found. The answer is that it is quite similar to the salvaging of unique American crafts such as old wooden flooring, great moldings, and fireplace façades. When a farmhouse or home deteriorates and a new structure is planned for the site, there are experts who evaluate the quality of craftsmanship and what can be salvaged. We work with professionals in many countries to locate these antiquities, and fortunately our steady demand for these products has produced a marvelous network of discriminating vendors.

The history of these tiles will lend a sense of charm and integrity to your home or garden project. These pieces are authentic; when the large wooden crates are opened, the tiles tell their history through the look and smell of delicate green moss—which is still growing on them! The antique terra-cottas from France are separated into divisions of blonde or dark, with the blonde colors ranging from very light tan to buckskin. These tiles unfortunately are quite precious and we struggle to keep up with the demand for this charming flooring. With antique terra-cotta, not only does color vary, but so do facial characteristics and edges, depending upon the age and origin of the material. The darker tiles range from light russet tones to deeper cordovan and are the more classic example of French tile found in the city and countryside.

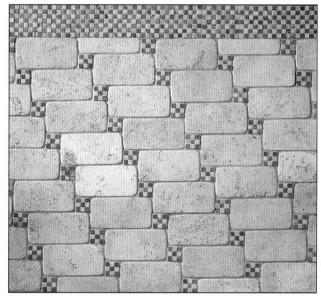

Top: This terra-cotta is reclaimed from French farmhouses and authenticated by the government to be at least 150 years old. Shown here is the rare blonde color mixed with the traditional russet—a stunning combination. ***Above:*** These lovely antiqued stone tiles, set in an exciting new variation of a traditional pattern, are popular because of their light, warm tones.

ART TILE

Handcrafted tile is a magnificent art form that is as dynamic today as at any time in history. Talented people all over the world are committed to personal artistic expression through glazed relief tiles, terra-cotta relief, hand-painted tiles, metal, glass, and mosaic. The mood is often historic, but the times in general are anything but conservative. Reproductions may be faithful, but reimagining, as in the case of metal and glass, is the energy that is driving the nineties. This energy could quite easily result in this being the richest tile decade of the twentieth century.

Above: A niche becomes a jeweled showcase for a luxurious selection of crackle- and luster-glazed, hand-crafted tile. *Right*: The elegant design of this contemporary kitchen is anchored by a splash of red and gold luster-glazed tiles, which feature a broad variation in shades due to ancient kiln firing techniques.

A kitchen done in neutral tones has the peacefulness associated with Grandmother's baking.
Butter-molded Meadow Vine tiles and borders form decorative panels on either side of the cooking
surface. Above the grill the Meadow Vine tiles, bordered with rustic and half-round liner bars,
frame a simple design of diagonally-placed pummeled marbled tiles.

Portuguese art tile is generously used indoors and outdoors on walls and building façades in Portugal. It is an enormous part of Portuguese art and architecture. Family dining on Sundays after church can take place in an awesome one-hundred-foot (30m) -high converted cathedral tiled up to and including the ceiling. In no other place in the world is the use of tile as passionate with pattern and color. Great stories are often told in murals that cover the walls, and one is surrounded by art, history, and theology. Stories told in tile are, of course, timeless. You can feel the power of the past and future in the drama of the tile itself as well as in the art created from tile.

The method by which these classic patterns are produced is quite simple. A process called pouncing involves powdered glazes being tapped into a pattern much like a doily that sits on the tile. Afterward the artisans, highly prized for their skill, paint over this faint outline and, with their brush strokes and colors, interpret this historic pattern.

Above: Custom relief tiles and murals can be rendered from original drawings, prints, or commercial designs, and are a good choice for a special or intimate location. This design is based on one of Walter Crane's illustrations for the Grimm tale "The Goose Girl." *Below, left to right:* A classic checkered pattern can be softened with a running vine border, while the introduction of stars into a primarily floral design adds a playful touch. European medallions can create elegance and a sense of timelessness in any room.

Left: The lovely hand-crafted tile
behind the stove is an example of the finest
of the traditional nineteenth-century
English art tile. Tile has been put to good
use in the rest of this kitchen as well—
note the countertops and the decorative edging
used on the counters and the hood over the
cooking area. *Above:* Handpainted tiles
are often made in traditional patterns and
colors (such as the tiles on the bottom row),
but they can be romantic (top right and
middle right) and even whimsical
(top left and middle left).

Top: The enchanting tiles that make up this stove surround were inspired by the sea. They add a playful touch of color that contrasts nicely with the soft-hued, worn brick in the rest of the kitchen.

Above: Fruit and vegetable patterns are favorites for decorating the kitchen. These handpainted tiles are reminiscent of folk art, and can help create a rustic decor.

Handpainted tiles can add a personal touch to your home. The owner of this kitchen has chosen tiles that complement the colors and patterns in the striking painting above the sink perfectly. Artistic and free-spirited designs in a range of colors and sizes can personalize even the most utilitarian spaces.

Top: Small tiles in solid colors may not be exciting on their own, but when several colors and shapes are used together the resulting patterns can be strikingly beautiful. *Above*: Simple geometric shapes can be combined to create strong, dramatic designs. *Opposite*: The richly hued multicolored tiles in this bathroom are dark when close to the floor and lighter near the ceiling, which makes the room seem larger and brighter than it actually is. The shower window trim is reminiscent of ancient tiled prayer niches, which lends a feeling of antiquity to this otherwise modern bath.

Handpainted tiles can be used to create beautiful murals, which are perfect for a backsplash or countertop in the kitchen or for a tabletop in a dining area.

This handpainted tile mural is so lovely that it is displayed as a work of art. The real bouquet in the folk-art pottery pitcher provides a charming contrast to the whimsical flowers painted on the tiles.

No discussion of art tile can be complete without an account of one of history's most passionate and challenging uses of tile as art in architecture: Antonio Gaudí's creation, Güell Park, in Barcelona, Spain.

Güell Park was originally conceived as a turn-of-the-century "bio-morphic, new wave" housing project planned by master Catalan architect Antonio Gaudí. Gaudí's unique body of work preceded that of Barcelona's other well-known sons, Pablo Picasso, Joan Miró, and Salvador Dali. The park is a curiosity,

This animal-head fountain in Market Hall exemplifies Gaudí's unique style of mosaic, which uses fragments of broken tiles to create the design, rather than the more traditional small, whole tiles.

"a maze of colorful ceramics and rustic stone," and Gaudí's architecture is perceived as a "private vision." The work was viewed as something that was disconnected from his own time as well as not connected to any past or future. However, in true Art Nouveau spirit, we see that Gaudí's "vision" brings into play the geometries of nature where a pure balance is found in a flurry of asymmetry.

Güell Park is home to one of the world's greatest tile structures, the Serpentine Bench, designed around 1912–1913 by Gaudí and his collaborator Josep Jujol. The bench is functional, decorative, imaginative, and accessible to everyone who visits the park. It is a piece of "built-in" outdoor furniture that traverses the full perimeter at the top of the Market Hall, a structure built to house a traditional weekly open-air market. The bench creates a tiled serpentine edge on the top of Market Hall, serving both as a sculpture and as a finish to the top of the building.

Gaudí and Jujol used material fragments from everywhere for the bench's mosaic surface work. Certain placements of glass, porcelain, unglazed pottery, cups, shells, plates, and even a porcelain doll's head were used to create color patterns and textured abstract shapes. The shading, toning, and patterning of the bench make it an irresistible object to touch, sit on, and admire. Viewing the bench or pictures of the bench will free anyone from the idea that there is 63a set of rules to apply to mosaic design. There are no design rules found in the work of the bench, no tradition save one: *trencadis*, the traditional Catalan decorative technique of shattering tile into fragments.

Left: A tremendous lizard fountain guards the stairs
that lead up to the Market Hall. Right: Sitting on top
of the Market Hall's columns is the Serpentine Bench.
New tiles were broken into fragments and then reassembled
and mortared into place in the bench; this technique is
called trencadis.

However, the Gaudí-Jujol technique used newly shaped and glazed tiles, which were then broken into fragments and reassembled in mortar in their original shape on a curved or warped surface. This method is one that Gaudí developed himself in the mid-1880s. Not only did the technique pave the way for the use of tile on convex and concave surfaces, it also allowed for great variations in color and shading: small pieces could be used to accessorize larger pieces by color or light refraction.

The *trencadis* used in the interior ceiling of the Market Hall was a deliberate installation for the purpose of indirect lighting. The specificity of artistic direction that was necessary to achieve the color variation in the tile shards is overwhelming. It has been found that the glaze, originally thought to be white, is instead a range of seventeen colors. Pale shades of green, blue, pink, and other hues are evident in the tile fragments. Today, such color customization can be achieved in only a few factories (for example, Ann Sacks Custom Color Factory in Portland, Oregon) and only by the most dedicated artisans.

PART TWO

STONE

Stone has been used as a building material since before history was recorded, and much of our own history can be traced through its use. Throughout the ages, stone has suggested grace, diversity, endurance, and sometimes mystery. It is one of the basic materials in our world, and its presence in castles, temples, and modest dwellings alike reveals all of its desirable qualities.

Ancient builders constructed monuments with a precision that rivals what we can achieve by contemporary methods; thus, we are in awe of the early reverence for stone. The five-ton (4.5t) carved stone monuments on Easter Island are one example. The culture so revered stones that each was imbued with an identity. Stones were also used as maps, often revealing directions to a hidden "key" that opened an

Opposite: Stonehenge is one of the world's most powerful symbols of duration and strength in architecture. The bluestones were so important to the ancient builders that they moved tremendous pieces over land and sea to bring them from Wales to England.

Above: Easter Island is famous for these colossal stone statues, which are situated on the slope of Rano Raraku, an extinct volcano.

Ahu Akivi, a grouping of seven megalithic carved stone statues on Easter Island. More than six hundred of these magnificent statues have been found on the island.

underground inner sanctum—a family treasure containing riches and idols.

The Irish and British revered stone as well. Stone structures of great architectural significance were built between 3700 and 3200 B.C. Five-ton (4.5t), cut-to-fit bluestone blocks from Wales were moved over land and water—a distance of more than three hundred miles (some 500km)—for the construction of the planetarium/observatory at Stonehenge. Early Mycenaeans (c. 1300 B.C.) built structures using jambs, thresholds, and twenty-five-ton (22.5t) stone lintels that held huge wooden doors in place.

We no longer use single twenty-five-ton (22.5t) lintels over entry posts, but our use of stone today reflects our appreciation for its dignity. Examples of stone's permanence are found in archways, stairways, balusters, and hearths. Today we may incorporate stone into the exteriors of our houses by way of our porches, patios, fences, and walks. And

stone is an unparalleled medium for interior spaces. An entryway of hand-chiseled stone pavers or a stone sink in a guest bathroom with stone-clad walls can bring us back to another time. Stone is at once peaceful and compelling.

If you are remodeling, think of installing stone cut to fit your kitchen countertop; for a less expensive alternative, purchase a smaller piece of marble, slate, or granite to use on a section of your existing countertop. This is an especially good surface for rolling out pastry dough and, because of its strength and durability, makes for a great chopping block as

well. Less porous than a butcher block, this is a safer and lower-maintenance alternative.

You may have considered making improvements to your master bath. Countertops and floors are the first places you may have thought of to use stone, but what about enclosing your tub with a granite facing? This type of renovation can totally change the

mood of your bath, and this material is available in several different colors. Black or white will give your room a contemporary feel, while a sandy or dusty rose tone will lend a European ambience.

The quality that stone suggests is disproportionate to its moderate cost, making it a great value and an excellent investment as an improvement to your home.

Opposite: The restrained use of color and bold selection of sizes and materials make this kitchen dramatic and extremely functional. Natural slate is very economical and maintenance free. *Above:* Pristine white towels, tub, and flowers complement the golden, warm tones of the stone used on the floor and in the tub surround. The natural variations in the color and texture of the stone create a classical look reminiscent of ancient Roman baths.

Some Types and Qualities of Stone

You may think of stone primarily in terms of its durability, or "hardness." Granite countertops, marble fireplaces, and slate floors seem to bring this to mind. But stone can also be soft, warm, and "absorbent," as well as mirrorlike. Limestone, for example, is a softer type of stone, and when used properly, this characteristic is apparent. To bring out the softness of limestone, combine various sizes of slabs. The distinctive sizes used in combination suggest a less formal arrangement. The cut of the stone will also affect its appearance. You may have your stone cut with "pillowed" or "cushioned" edges, in which the undulating, untreated surface edges are finished in a downward curve; as the name implies, the resulting piece of stone looks like a pillow.

Stone can be subject to different types of treatment by which different effects are achieved. It can be polished, honed, flamed, or acid-washed to fit your design needs. Each treatment presents another opportunity for you to get a feeling for how you would like to use this material.

Being informed about different kinds of stone and how they are formed will help you to better use the material in your home's design. Following is a sampling of different types of stone and their qualities and characteristics.

A calibrated stone means that each piece will be uniform, giving a more formal appearance. Polished stone is mirrorlike and honed smooth but has a matte finish. A flamed limestone has a rough, natural texture. Acid-washed stone has a feeling of softness and informality.

Opposite: Antiquities blend artfully with American craft in this stunning bath design. Especially charming is the rare blonde antique terra-cotta from France, which forms the diagonal-set wainscoting. The warm, creamy tones on the upper walls create a splendid background for the butter-molded, handcrafted tile trim. *Above*: Hand-set stones are used to re-create historical designs. Here, limestone and terra-cotta are cut into small pieces suitable for mosaics.

Left: Clean white tiles on the walls brighten this kitchen, while the rugged limestone floor gives it a touch of old-world charm. *Top*: Honed, matte-finished yellow and white Del Veneto limestones with a gray drop-in border make a formal pattern. Fossils appear at random. *Above*: Combining irregular tile sizes and shapes can add depth and softness to a space, creating a casual feeling.

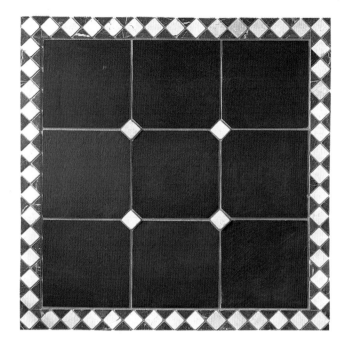

Above: Fine-grained dark gray slate in subtle, natural, textured surfaces is elegant when combined with white diagonal insets and borders. *Below*: Color variation in slate ranges from sandy hues with traces of rose or gray to vibrant golden and bronze tones to rich, dark green, russet, and silver-gray. *Opposite*: Slate splits easily into slabs. Here, copper slate is inset with a herringbone pattern and hand-crafted metal tiles.

The potential applications of stone vary a great deal depending on its natural characteristics, including hardness, density, and water absorption. As with all rules, though, there are exceptions. Limestone is less suitable than granite and domestic slate for exterior use in climates with freezing temperatures. You may sometimes use these materials in freezing conditions, but proper installation is critical and the thickness of the material must be increased to strengthen it. A professional showroom and contractor should be involved in such a selection.

Limestone is marvelous for varied architectural styles. Its neutrality and subtlety are perfect for avoiding the possibility of over-ornamentation. Many limestones from Europe are a light, creamy color, relatively unfigured, and fabricated in shapes ranging from 12" by 12" (30 by 30cm) tiles to solid columns, archways, benches, stairs, tabletops, and counters. Limestone is also a highly desirable flooring material. Its simple elegance is most notable in mosaics and other elaborate border designs.

Portugal produces beautiful limestone and marbles. The most well-known limestones are the Alpinia Clara and Alpinia Rosada, as well as the yellow-gold Amarelo Dos Negrais. Some, like the Braco Rosal and the Xita stone, are on the pink side. For a brownish hue, Portugal has Breccia Portuguesa and Breccia Tavira Dourada, and for a red-brown coloration, Breccia Lioz and Breccia Tavira Bermila. A white-clear stone is Branca Rosal, and a lovely soft gray-blue stone is the Vidraco De Ataija. Portuguese marble is exquisite: Estremos Vergades is a beautiful white stone, and Estremos Vergades Castanhas is a white stone with a brownish tint. A marble with a white-gray tone is the Ruivina Clara, and a deeper gray marble is the Ruivina Escura. Portugal also produces wonderful green marble: there are Verde Viana Claro, Cristal, and Escuro, which range from light, springtime green to an elegant emerald shade.

Opposite: Warm, golden biblical stone covers this shower from floor to ceiling. Combining two sizes of stone squares creates visual interest. *Below:* Vanilla-colored marble covers the magnificent round tub and surround in this luxurious Roman-style bathroom. Matching tiles cover the walls, and a handsome x-bench adds to the Neoclassical mood.

Above: Designs in antiqued stone can create a
feeling of elegance and history in any room.
Below: Earthy colors and patterns such as these
are timeless and provide endless design possibilities. *Opposite*: This copper tub is in an appropri-
ately rich and antique setting, surrounded with
tumbled golden stone flooring and split antique
biblical stone that covers the walls from floor to
ceiling. The warm rose and russet tones in the
stone echo the colors in the dark copper bath.

Italy's famous pure white Carrara marble is the
best-known marble. It is a high-demand stone and a
true classic. Other types of stone from Italy's quarries
are the lovely yellow-gold (*giallo*) marble Avoria
Siena, Italy's high-quality travertines, Caesar (Roman
Classic) and Caesar Fieure, and the well-known light
travertine Navona. Versace Limestone, an acid-washed,
light-colored stone, is a beautiful material from Central
America. This stone can be cut with either a "cushion"
edge, which gives it a softer, warmer appearance, or a
straight edge, which is ideal for more precise installations. It is figured much like a French limestone but at
a lower cost, and a wide variety of custom sizes and
shapes is available.

Although it seems unlikely, you can install stones
that have been treated with an acid wash or pummeled
to appear thousands of years old. They are available
in geometric patterns and can be coordinated for installation with other larger-format "antiqued" stones. The
"antiqued" stones are pummeled marble or travertine,
and become ancient-looking after the processing.

A narrow galley kitchen becomes an inspirational artistic statement with the use of tumbled stone on the counter and apron, and rustic Patel-patterned mosaics on the back-splash. The mosaics are formed from pieces that were cut and split from ancient limestone flooring that came from Israel.

Adriatic and Hebron mosaics are made in the oldest tradition. These stones are treated to appear as ancient as the famous installations in Rome. Guilloche, Lotus, and Patel border patterns are easy to install on their mesh mounting and perfect for use in conjunction with plain or patterned field tile.

Ancient biblical stone from the Middle East, certified to be between five hundred and one thousand years old, has become available in North America exclusively through Ann Sacks Tile and Stone. The lovely butter-smooth surface of this stone reveals the patina and undulations from wear. Colors vary from ocher to cream to russet. The material comes from Israel and is found in random sizes and thickness, depending on the scale of the home or building from which it has been salvaged.

Each stone in an Aegean mosaic is a different natural color taken from the palette of quarry stones, and each individual stone brings its own hue and texture to the mosaic. The idea that stone is a "cold" material rapidly disappears as these designs illustrate that stone can offer softness and warmth. A mosaic with an acid-washed Versace limestone field surrounded by a border pattern of Aegean mosaics is a design as warm and inviting as a medieval tapestry. This stonework is especially suited to verandas, foyers, or sunrooms—wherever you welcome your guests.

Above: This is a classic Hebron plain mosaic with a Cypress-patterned border. *Below*: These border designs are paired with antique field mosaics, which exhibit less texture and smoother surfaces than a classic field mosaic.

A stylized wave, a classic guilloche, and the whimsical Patel motif are but a few of the border patterns that can provide a striking accent to a simple tile wall or floor.

DESIGNING A MOSAIC FLOOR

Here we have captured the story of the development of mosaic art at Ann Sacks. Earlier this year we received from a valued client a rendering of a classic European mosaic floor. What you see is the process by which we turned this creative idea into a magnificent and authentic mosaic floor to be installed in a luxury hotel.

Below, left: The first section of the floor is created using architectural drawings that we produced to scale. *Below, right:* The finished medallion section and a close-up of the installed piece reveal the lovely hand-crafted character. *Opposite:* The various stages of development of each pattern in the design that will be repeated.

The Power and Permanence of Stone

In all its varied uses, stone embodies celebration, rituals, and memories. Stone is used in both classical and innovative designs and always represents permanence and craftsmanship. This is apparent at once when you make the decision to use slate, marble, or limestone in your home. The selection of stone for its texture and strength and the placement of stone are artistic tasks that have been performed from the beginning of time. Designing with stone creates great opportunities for learning from the past and realizing possibilities for the future. Combining ancient carved stone with rustic terra-cotta or sleek polished slabs with steel and glass takes you on a journey through time.

Every language, including architecture, evolves as a variation on a theme. Gradual variations in the use of stone included painting the surfaces of stones and setting them out to dry before they were put into place. Sometimes, if they were exterior materials,

Below, left: A Roman field mosaic with a ribbon border reflects light from a multitude of surfaces. *Below, right:* Tiny stones in a variety of natural hues were used to create this delicate mosaic, which is in the Citadel in Jerusalem. *Opposite:* The variety of sizes and shapes in the limestone floor of this cozy breakfast nook complements the lovely detailed woodwork.

the stones were colored after they were installed. It is presumed that this activity led to the improvisational shaping of pieces of mud or clay to be used as they were needed to create mosaics. Individual pieces were painted and set out to bake in the sun. Whether painted or unpainted, the baked clay pieces became an important stepping-stone in the evolving language of architecture.

Right: An edged stone counter with an inlaid grapevine and leaf in classic, smooth Adriatic mosaic is set off by the soft ocher walls, which are covered with antique stone. *Below, left:* A stunning reproduction of an ancient Adriatic mosaic floor medallion is made in sea-washed hues. *Below, right:* A mosaic medallion shows that "neutral" tones come in a very wide range.

THE LOUVRE

A fine example of a good partnership of materials and design can be seen in a recent architectural challenge: the addition to the Louvre in Paris. Additions are by nature difficult, particularly when the original structure is itself a historical treasure and monument, and the architectural achievement of the addition has to be related in some way to the original building.

The glass pyramid, designed by I.M. Pei, presented a great contrast in architectural styles and left the architectural relationship between the original building and the new addition somewhat elusive. What, then, could possibly be the unifying element? What could pull these two different moments in architecture into one purposeful statement?

Pei tied the ancient regime to the modern by filling the place with indigenous, creamy-white limestone. The stone represented centuries of French culture; its neutrality and simple elegance were familiar to the French, and it is a reminder to everyone that the original architecture of the Louvre is as much a part of the present as is the new addition. In this case, the power of stone united the present to the past in a project that will surely be treated with the reverence due fine art.

The glass pyramid in the Cour Napoleon welcomes visitors to the Louvre Museum in Paris, France.

PART THREE

TILE & STONE IN THE HOME

Tile and stone are beautiful, durable materials that can impressively change the look of your home. Whether you choose to totally revamp your decor or just want to incorporate a delightful finishing touch, these materials will make great additions to your exterior and interior spaces. This section will give you ideas for every room in your home, as well as for your garden paths, pergolas, porches, and pools.

Opposite: The random patterning of a Versace limestone floor lends an antique French flavor to this bathroom. Simple white tile "bricks" complement the irregular but geometric design of the floor.

My Favorite Application

Has there ever been a time when you thought that your living room or family room needed a refurbishing but the job seemed too big or too expensive? You probably couldn't escape the feeling that there must be a solution—one that wouldn't overly tax your life or your bank account. In this situation my first option for change is the flooring—something that improves the actual structure of the house. This improvement contributes beauty, eases maintenance, and in the long run delivers the greatest value. While we will be moving on soon to a discussion of smaller changes, or what are sometimes called "points of expression," I would like to take this time to briefly discuss the value of installing a hard surface as flooring.

Not only is properly selected tile or stone a change that can substantially express a style in your home, it will also add greatly to the quality and clean appearance of any room. Practically without exception,

Left, top and bottom, and top right: Economical glazed tiles from Italy stand up to wear and still reflect the rustic and aesthetic traditions of the Italian culture. *Below, right:* French antique Parefeuille terra-cotta is a substantial, durable flooring material that is perfect for carefree living. *Opposite:* A carefully chosen stone floor may be the only change you need to make to update your kitchen. Here, rich multicolored slate is set off by stunning metal inserts, which match the drawer pulls.

tile or stone flooring, including relatively soft and elegant limestones, can be mopped or even hosed when provided with proper drainage. Today's sealants combat staining and stand up very well to moisture. With this one change your house can feel like the homes of Europe, which for centuries have had their original tile floors. In fact, these precious floors (even the most pedestrian terra-cottas) are salvaged when the houses can no longer stand and are resold all over the world to provide many more years of beauty and utility! This is a testimony not only to their strength but to their timeless aesthetic appeal. What carpet, vinyl, or even wood available today can provide hundreds of years of service and be even more desirable afterward? This is why, if you have never lived with tile or stone floors, I urge you to consider that single change when you want to upgrade the quality and beauty of your home forever.

Points of Expression

Look at a plain doorway inside your home. It could be the doorway that leads from the dining room to the kitchen. There's probably nothing special about it; it is just your passage to the next room. You have passed through this doorway an endless number of times and never felt that it had character or welcomed you. Step back and look at the doorway: does it visually bring you into the room? If not, it is missing the opportunity to be a gateway from one room to another and set a tone at eye level for your home. With tile, you could create a memorable passage with a theme, and thus improve the vitality of both rooms at a very nominal cost in time and money. And you could have a wonderful time doing it! This is a pragmatic trick that Europeans have used for centuries and part of the charm that attracts us to the rustic homes of Italy and France. It is not only a wonderful touch for the wealthy; it is a measure of creativity and love of the home within the reach of any homeowner.

Left: The earthy tones of these tiles create a warm, soft variation on a traditional Islamic basketweave pattern. *Opposite:* Biblical stone pavers from Israel replace standard wood flooring in this striking home. Textural, warm, and compelling, they transform this home into a great treasure.

Perhaps you were browsing a tile showroom this past week and you fell in love with a tile—an 8" (20cm) glazed earthenware hand-molded tile with a figure of a running rabbit. It captured your heart but you didn't think you had an appropriate place to use it. What about that doorway? Begin by tiling around the door frame with a complementary field tile. The large rabbit tiles might be placed at the top center of the doorway or at each corner. Your ordinary doorway has now become a whimsical, welcoming entry.

Use this trick at other points in your home, changing the style of design from one location to another. Each time your result will be original and fresh. You may want to create a door surround for the front door as a greeting to guests, or around the doorway of each bedroom. Just imagine, each time someone enters a room in your home, they will encounter a special moment—your own way of saying "welcome."

Stretch this technique of expression past doorways. Maybe you have just moved into a new house with one or more fireplaces that are fairly new and don't need to be replaced, but are also quite austere. There are several ways to bring that small space to life. You might fit the fireplace with architectural ceramic tiles in terra-cotta or rustic stoneware. Or you may select a design using a combination of custom deco tiles along the mantel with similarly colored field tiles along the sides of the fireplace. The side treatment may also be punctuated with an occasional deco tile.

Opposite: Rough gray stones are a perfect counterbalance for the delicate, handpainted ceramics in this English-style bathroom.
Above: The diamond-patterned marble border on the wall of this bathroom provides an elegant contrast to the rugged stone floor.

A fireplace surround is the perfect point of expression. Everything about it is critical to the feeling of your home. It is symbolic of warmth and gathering; it is physically central to the room that is usually designated for family and guest activities; and it is typically symmetrical, which is ideal for applications of tile and stone. There is no limit to the creative opportunities for your fireplace, and

Opposite: This fabulous room illustrates the strength and character that can be achieved with the generous use of stone. The random-patterned flooring is antique limestone that has been reclaimed from a London residence. *Above:* This beautiful fireplace takes its inspiration from the Arts and Crafts movement. Smoky green tiles in varying shapes set off oak leaf and acorn borders, and mythological animals surround the opening of the fireplace. Warm terra-cotta colors on the floor provide an accent to the cool greens and blues of the fireplace.

because the quantity of tile used is quite modest, you can fall in love without breaking the bank.

This is the area where you can take the simplest decorative concepts of your home and focus them so that there is a single passionate expression of a style that you love. For the traditionalist there is the quiet art of Dutch hand-painted tile, which can add quality and European style to a simple Colonial home. Stoneware handcrafted in matte or deep transparent crackle glazes clearly says "English" or "Arts and Crafts" in even the smallest installation.

Maybe you have a wall in your yard or a garden without a path. The setting of these points of expression is perfect for the addition of small murals or mosaic compositions, which can enliven sections of your wall that may occasionally be "lost" in shade or foliage. If you do install a path, try using antique terra-cotta tiles with grasses growing between them. Don't bother to remove the moss that is on them when they arrive unless you are concerned about slipperiness. Allowing the moss to remain on the sides and less used stones keeps them looking as they did on the French patio from which they were salvaged.

Tile and stone are versatile materials that can be used throughout your home—both inside and out—to beautify your surroundings and give your home a sense of timelessness. This section of the book has been designed to give you fresh ideas and new inspiration to use these materials throughout your home's decor.

Above: This garden wall boasts a fountain that looks centuries old—it is earthy and dramatic at the same time. **Opposite**: The glazed terra-cotta tiles paving this front walkway hint at the beauty that will be revealed once you are inside the home.

Exteriors

Exterior areas are good places to consider using tile and stone. In addition to imbuing spaces with elegance and solidity, they are more durable and will stand up to the demands of time and harsh elements better than other materials such as wood and iron, which are prone to rot or rust.

GARDEN PATHS AND WALKWAYS

In designing and building a garden path, function alone does not determine that you use a particular type of tile or stone. You will also want your path or walkway to mirror the mood of your garden in certain ways. The formal patterning of terra-cotta may be right in an English-style yard, while mosaics are the richest complement to a historic Italianate house or terrace.

Your home is your respite from the hectic world. In urban areas, a garden is a welcome relaxation spot. In Japan, the garden path, or *roji*, is

Opposite: This outdoor terrace is transformed into a timeless garden with the addition of rustic stone pavers and a lovely, intricately patterned tile fountain. The lush plants and the carved stone bench add to the feeling of being in paradise.

designed to signify a primary stage of meditation, which is intended to break the connection with the outside world and to produce a fresh sensation conducive to the full enjoyment of aestheticism. It is designed to offer a safe passage to self-illumination. Of course, the placement and types of materials that you choose may only serve as a map for those traveling over your pathway.

Granite or slate stepping-stones fitted tightly together create a smooth pavement for a brisk walk through the garden. By simply separating the stones with irregular and wider spacing (planted with moss or thyme, perhaps), you will find that the path is one you'll slow your pace to walk on.

The best path or walkway uses stone and tile in concert and is immensely enjoyable to build. For example, if you are working with limestone, travertine, or antique terra-cotta pavers as the primary path material and they are ready for installation, you might select a group of small glazed or unglazed tiles, pebbles, glass tiles, or shells to be used as accents. These smaller pieces can be randomly or carefully placed into your path to create a lovely personal expression of greeting.

Generally, the tiles used today for paving paths and walkways are some type of terra-cotta, and are frost-proof for locations that have snow. They are made of clay and fired to a high temperature, enabling them to withstand more wear and exposure than certain softer-bodied natural tiles or more slippery and vulnerable glazed ones. Terra-cotta tile is especially suited to outdoor areas: it can be sealed to prevent damage from the elements, and its warm, natural palette of colors provides a quiet background to the brilliant flowers and lush grasses and greenery.

This walkway is both expressive and personal. No straight lines or traditional uses of material are found here, and the flying bird adds yet another touch of whimsy.

Natural stone is also a favorite material for paths, including the beautifully pummeled marble and travertine imports. Travertine sidewalks and pathways are reminscent of the narrow Roman avenues walked on by sandaled ancients. Small stone tiles (usually 2" by 2" [5 x 5cm] or 4" by 4" [10 by 10cm] with a small triangular-shaped tile to be used for the border) are available in all the tones that nature provides, including white, gray, black, gold, rich brown, russet, pink, cream, and a beautiful palette of greens.

Whether you are designing with granite, limestone, travertine, slate, or tile, it is important that you consider the qualities and characteristics of the material you choose. Paths and walkways create shifts in perspective; they move a person from one place to another both physically and, in part, psychologically. The design of the walkway leading to your house establishes a "rhythm" and should extend a feeling of hospitality to guests as they approach your threshold.

PERGOLAS

We may be only slightly aware of the transition that occurs on an open walkway between the garden and the house. A pergola is a simple yet valuable structure used to achieve a gradual introduction and entry to a porch or sunroom and makes a perfect point of expression for your personal vision.

The visual unity between the outdoor area and the main house can be carried in the lines of the pergola, as well as in the materials used in the architecture of the main building. The door and window framing and architectural integrity of the house can be extended in every direction with a minimum of labor and materials. The pergola itself is probably made of wood planks or metal framing. The overhead planks are designed to fit a certain distance from each other in order to allow ample room for large-vined plants to weave in between the beams. In the case of a large plant, such as wisteria, the spaces and structure must be able to accommodate the continuously growing strength of the woody-trunked vine. Here, however, is a terrific opportunity for the natural characteristics of tile or stone to be used to pull together the elements in one of the most elusive yet elegant spaces in your environment.

The overhead structural frame and the side posts of the pergola rely heavily on the paving and flooring material to define the character of the space. A glazed tile floor will make the space seem more like an interior part of the house. Stone pavers or quarry tiles will maintain the feeling of the outdoors in this setting. Visualize what the space will look like in the off-season—when the leaves are off the vines and the pergola frame is exposed. During this period the beauty and durability of the floor are especially critical for sustaining the outdoor-to-indoor transition.

PORCHES

The splendor and simplicity that stone brings to walkways and entries have made stone the choice of architects for every type of building, from the tiniest summer house to great mansions and public buildings. The porch uses these materials for similar design purposes.

A distinctive stone structure, the stoa was designed by Greek architects in the late seventh century B.C. as a sanctuary. Selecting the most modest and available material of the time—stone—the stoa was first intended as an overnight shelter for travelers and pilgrims. Over time, it evolved into a public

The autumn leaves set into the floor of this entryway are bordered with Aegean quarry stones. The nature-inspired pattern and earthy hues make this a perfect transitional space between the outdoors and the inside of the house.

space in the home, accommodating activities such as public sessions, banquets, and the posting of notices.

Today, porches are gathering places that provide a pleasant sense of intimacy in the intermediate space between the indoors and the outdoors. Large porches offer many opportunities for using tile and stone decoration. Stairs that lead to the porch may be transformed with slate or quartz tile. A doorway that opens onto a balcony can be made more inviting with the addition of art tile surrounding the opening. Time spent on the porch is leisure time—perhaps an aesthetic respite—so porches are ideal places to install tile murals or relief tiles surrounding painted floral pictures. Hexagonal or triangular shapes and uniquely shaped glazed tiles add a lovely dimension as a framing device for a mural. Around the turn of the century, the British took up the habit of using small murals and sets of decorative relief tiles at entrances for the brief entertainment of guests waiting for the door to be opened.

There are many considerations when selecting a flooring material for a porch. In America it has been most common with wooden homes to also use wood for the flooring of the porch. This was probably done to extend the house "out" effortlessly with no break in color or texture. While aesthetically this is a pleasing approach, it is not ideal in climates with extremes of cold, heat, or moisture. Expansion and contraction caused by freezing and thawing warps boards and creates gaps, and heat and moisture require the wood to be painted. Moisture also leads to dry rot, which left untreated can damage the home itself. A stone or terra-cotta porch has none of these drawbacks and can be linked to the house very successfully. Neutral stones such as limestone are elegant; slates are extraordinarily durable and simple enough to work into almost any architecture; and terra-cottas are frost-proof, can be rustic or sleek, and have nonskid stain treads.

The whimsical details of this otherwise traditional patio are perfect against the dramatic view. Autumn leaves in muted colors are set off by matte terra-cotta tiles, and a rough stone birdbath contrasts nicely with the more delicately carved balustrade.

POOLS

The swimming pool presents the homeowner with exciting opportunities in which to use tile and stone. In the days of antiquity, tiling a pool was a means to seal the structure from leakage, but present technology doesn't limit the use of tile. Today it is as decorative as it is functional.

Tile and stone are often used for pool decking. A certain amount of care is required when selecting a good and safe decking material. A textured stone or tile is a good choice. Look for a material that has heat-

A classic checkerboard design of black and turquoise tiles provides a striking accent to the understated pale terra-cotta flooring and simple furnishings of this sunny pool deck.

reflecting properties as well as skid resistance. Plant moss or Corsican mint between the stones to create additional traction and relate to surrounding greenery.

Decorate your pool with tile from the bottom up. Refracted sunlight passing through the water will beautifully reflect tile designs on the pool floor. The variety of tile patterns found on floors is absolutely fantastic! A simple line to keep a lap swimmer on the right track may be all that is desired, or perhaps a tiled edge and just a few tiled risers on the pool steps for a minimalist decorative touch is appropriate. An alternative approach is to create a pattern as vivacious as the water is still. Consider the illusion of precious stones scattered across the pool's floor or glass mosaics depicting classic Roman sea themes. The glass mosaic tiles come in a larger variety of colors

than stone pieces and have a deeper color range than ceramic tile. And glass tiles are brilliant and reflective in shimmering water.

Tile and stone designs on pool decking are used as traffic directions, sidewalks, or paths leading to the pool house or other areas on the grounds. These designs can either share the pattern started at the pool or diverge from it. You can also incorporate tile designs into one or two interior wall panels of the pool house. If the house has an open side facing the pool, the back wall of the pool house may be a perfect place for a mosaic backdrop or a lovely tile pattern. Vertical ornamentation near a pool works like outdoor sculpture in blending the art of both nature and humans.

The many subtle shades of blue in the tiles surrounding the pools of this fountain echo the colors of the water and sky. The strong impact made by the use of a single color balances the elegant architecture and grand scale of this home.

Interiors

Any home's interior will be transformed with the use of tile or stone. Durability is the added benefit here, as the materials you choose will last as long as your home.

Opposite: Rare blonde antique terra-cotta from France is used here with reclaimed wood to create a traditional European-style entry. *Below:* Honed natural stone stands up to all uses and all design challenges—a fabulous material for architects.

ENTRYWAYS

Entries and foyers are a first glimpse into your home. A hand-carved wooden door illustrates both the inhabitants' interest in crafts and the dedication of the carver. Such a door provides an invitation to come inside and enjoy a world of new experiences. Similarly, a beautiful floor expresses a personal welcome.

An entry designed in a classical theme is soothing and familiar. Flooring material here may be a neutral-colored marble or limestone with a border of contrasting stone running around the perimeter of the area.

This entry will give one a sense that the inner workings of the home are structured and orderly. An entry with a mosaic or a pattern of autumn leaves in earthy hues sets an entirely different tone—expressive and promising more detail and creativity to follow. Like the door, this sends a message about love of art.

Buildings not originally intended as permanent living spaces have sometimes been converted into studios or summer houses. Your house may have originally been a stable or a carriage house, and therefore the floor may be made of rough and uneven stone pavers. This flooring suggests the earthiness of the country, where trips from the vegetable garden to the kitchen are not discouraged just because of the mud brought into the home.

Above: These tiles, with their earthy patterns reminiscent of pressed flowers, would be an ideal accent to a rough stone floor in a foyer.

SUNROOMS

The sunroom has a wide variety of uses in contemporary living. It may function as a sanctuary for tender plant species or as a quiet reading room or dining room. Sunroom structures vary widely, particularly between those that were configured in the original house design and those added later.

Quarry tiles or small glazed floor tiles are perfect for the sunroom. A floor comprised of flagstone or limestone accentuates the natural sunlight, greenery, and comfortable furnishings and offsets the simple elegance of terra-cotta pots. Aside from their decorative value, the functionality of tile and stone in the sunroom is unmatched—these materials capture and store the heat of the sun. This creates a thermal condition in the sunroom, which plays a major role in maintaining the good health of plants.

If you are planning to use your sunroom as a multipurpose area for family relaxation or dining, your flooring material will be an equally valuable asset to you in achieving temperature control. If you are able to position your room in the correct way to allow the angles of the sun to come in the windows at a high point and not reach the floor, your floor will be cooler than the room's air temperature. This is a wonderful, practical advantage that tile and stone can add to your home.

Opposite: Warm Spanish terra-cotta flooring and a comfortable woven-seat chair make this sunroom the perfect place to relax and play a game of chess.

THE GREAT ROOM

Reminiscent of bygone eras, contemporary homes are being designed with "great rooms" as opposed to separate living rooms, family rooms, kitchens, and dining areas. These rooms embody a sense of shared family life and nurture the family's sense of well-being.

The architecture of the great room commands a multidimensional open space of high or vaulted ceilings, pass-through views, and plenty of natural light. It is the primary area for indoor activity: alcoves for watching television and videos, for cooking and dining, and for reading can be found in the great room. Stairways and landings that run along the edges of the room and lead to private quarters— bedroom and bathing areas—may open onto a two- or three-story atrium that offers a view of the entire room. A more formal architectural design for the great room might include a combination of living room, dining room, and sunroom that would accommodate plenty of guests for large dinner parties, cocktail parties, and holiday events. Fireplaces and wet bars, surface treatments, window framing, wall cladding, and flooring are all composite parts of the utility of the space. The great room offers many opportunities in which to use tile and stone as you make your design choices.

Creating design themes and patterns will help to make subtle distinctions between the personal and common areas of this room. For example, you may choose a pillow-cut limestone tile as the primary flooring material. The kitchen area could be defined by installing a border pattern in the limestone that rings the kitchen and continues around the entire great room. When the border approaches the reading alcove, it might end and another might begin with a simple, offset pattern of "drop-ins." The border pattern can resume on the other side of the reading alcove and continue its path around the room. Creating spatial distinctions with these patterns is similar to the concept of using an actor's "mark" onstage: it serves to guide activities.

Staircases that overlook the great room invite the use of several types of spatial patterning. Movement and direction can be emphasized here with colorful tile or mosaic patterns on the cap of the stair railing. Perspective on the area covered by the staircase is determined by the width of vertical pattern and the color used on the risers. The elevation of the climb and its duration are indicated by the width and material choices of the stair tread. For example, a scrappy, intermittent mosaic of color splashes on and near the railing cap might indicate

Opposite: A room with multiple functions uses tile and stone to delineate activities. The kitchen work area is distinguished by a simple white backsplash with a floral corner pattern. The cooking area takes on a professional demeanor with copper cookware accentuated by dark antique terra-cotta.

that following the stairs would lead one to additional common and informal spaces; a solid tile in a more uniform color pattern might indicate a formal, possibly "off-limits" area.

Stair risers with narrow tile or granite strips in a graduating range of colors create the illusion of a short trek. This impression could be entirely reversed by placing broad, uniform-in-color stone or ceramic tiles on

Opposite: Antique terra-cotta from Bali is absolutely stunning in this new yet rustic villa-style home. It was selected for its ability to stand up to a busy country lifestyle. *Above*: Sleek, modern, and original, this limestone floor is handsomely detailed with ceramic spirals and metal squares. The fireplace is also a superb combination of stone, tile, and metal.

the risers. Using a matte or flat-finish tile on the stair treads slows the action, and a long, leisurely climb with the implication of discovering an inviting and comfortable surprise at the top of the staircase is indicated.

The great room offers an opportunity to use tile and stone designs in textures and motifs that can reappear in a thematic, romantic sense in every corner of your home and property.

Simple, white, rectangular European tiles are used to cover one wall of this dining room. The tiles echo the shapes of the painted bricks of the fireplace, and their clean, glossy white surface sets off the wonderful pottery from Spain, Italy, and America.

KITCHENS

Traditional uses of tile and stone in kitchens were born in response to the need for a nonporous surface material for food preparation. Kitchen surface materials also need to be impervious to and have a capacity for channeling water.

Early European kitchens featured large basins carved from marble or stone slabs. A molded terra-cotta "pipe" was connected to a drain hole in the wall that funneled water outside. The weight of the basin was sufficient enough to form a seal at the contact points with surrounding edges of the thick wooden blocks used as counters. This seal prevented water from

The raised grapevine tiles bordering the sink are only one element of the playful fruit theme employed in this kitchen.

coming into contact with the wood and helped avoid water damage and deterioration of the counter structure. Tile and stone backsplashes were also designed to protect cabinet and wall joints from water damage.

But the utilitarian functions of tile and stone in kitchens went beyond water protection. Safety concerns were also allayed with these materials. Around ovens and stoves, for example, tile and stone

Opposite: Hand-painted blue-and-white tiles from Portugal are perfect for a traditional, functional, light kitchen. Surprisingly economical, these classic tiles can be found with very little decoration, or can be intensely patterned, as seen on Lisbon's ancient avenues. *Above*: This kitchen is a country haven, with a tile folk-art landscape above the stove top and the countryside rolling along the countertops in the backsplash design.

installations provided a protective guard against heat for floors and walls. The wall was protected from heat damage when an oven was set atop a tile or stone base.

A contemporary variation of the utility of these materials can be found in decorative yet functional examples. A floor-to-ceiling installation of tiles in random solid colors behind the oven and stove top will serve to protect the wall from heat damage and create a framed design for the cooking area. The effect is that of a place in motion, a busy area that

Above: Marvelous handmade tiles in the tradition of Middle Eastern ceramic art create a focal point in this rustic and extremely charming kitchen. *Opposite:* A generous use of the classic octagon-and-dot pattern is the key to this traditional kitchen. A raised grapevine border decorates the stove's hood.

does not invite additional activity and distinguishes the area and the tasks that are performed there from those in other areas of the kitchen.

Another use for tile and stone in the kitchen that may not be obvious at first is to aid in gardening. Due to its warmth and humidity, the kitchen is ideally suited to starting plant growth and for the continued healthy life of some mature plants. Kitchen window gardeners rely on tile and stone surfaces under plants for easy maintenance along with the thermal qualities of solar heat retention and humidity modification. The combination of tile, light, and heat can create a moderately manageable microclimate in your kitchen.

Opposite: This festive, graphic use of handcrafted tile looks just as it would in a charming kitchen in Provence. The red marble countertop is perfect for rolling out homemade pasta dough.

Above: Red and gold luster-glazed tiles create a striking backsplash for this sink.

In addition to functional purposes, tile and stone can be used to create beauty and balance in the kitchen. These materials can be used to mediate natural light by capturing all of the available morning sunlight or dissipating the glaring afternoon light. The installation of high-gloss glazed tiles, ranging from 1" by 1" (2.5 by 2.5cm) to 4" by 4" (10 by 10cm), will reflect the incoming light, brightening the space. In areas where morning or afternoon light is too bright, this light can be "screened" by installing patterns of alternating larger square tiles that have matte or unglazed finishes on kitchen countertops and floors. The lighting will be balanced, rather than too bright in one area and too dark in another. This screened

Left and above: This is a superb illustration of the use of tile as art. A beautiful mosaic tree, custom made in Israel, becomes the stunning focal point of this kitchen.

lighting allows the decorative tiles you have chosen to take center stage.

Other places in the kitchen that are ideal for displaying decorative tiles are backsplashes, "place mats" installed on a counter eating area, and cutting surfaces on an island. These can have various designs, such as blocks of color, broken or pattern mosaic designs, or granite and marble inlays. Additional innovative tile work in the kitchen might include a ceiling molding of relief border tiles.

Above: The soft pastel hues and calming, easy patterns etched into the backsplash tiles of this contemporary kitchen make it a peaceful, pleasant place to cook. *Opposite:* Handmade stoneware tiles are both beautiful and durable enough for counters in a busy family kitchen. Bright, cheerful colors enliven the backsplash and stove hood, which has a Victorian floral border.

Opposite: Exposed brick creates a rustic surround for this kitchen range. The forest green
and terra-cotta tiles behind the stove add a Mediterranean flavor. *Above:* The lovely, understated
tiles of Valencia, Spain, are the perfect neutral backdrop for the plates with botanical motifs
and the handmade pottery in this rustic kitchen.

BEDROOMS

Bedrooms that are designed with tile and stone are most often found in houses in sunny and tropical zones, or in summer and beach houses. Two of the primary reasons for using these materials in bedrooms that have plenty of sun are temperature control and light modulation.

You may find it necessary to plan carefully in order to achieve a perfect morning temperature and brightness in your bedroom. Planning for these conditions will help you determine which materials are most appropriate. Both tile and stone are efficient solar collectors, so the orientation of the room will determine whether or not you use these materials in your bedroom.

For your floor, a cushioned or undulating surface might be desirable. A pillow-cut limestone, glazed or unglazed terra-cotta tile, or biblical stone will evoke the feeling of walking barefoot along the beach. You may want to continue the installation of the flooring material though a doorway or French windows to an outside porch or terrace. If you plan to grow plants in the window well, tile the windowsills and frames inside as well as outside.

Another option for using tile and stone in the bedroom is to adorn your headboard and bed surround with a tile design. The tiles may be made of stone with a patterned border or of glazed ceramic or unglazed quarry tile.

Opposite: The walls of this romantic bedroom are reproductions of the beautiful stone walls built in France in the seventeenth century. *Above:* Soft, lovely tumbled stone is used here to create a wall detail reminiscent of ancient Europe.

Stone or marble fireplaces are often used in the bedroom. Their curved design is reminiscent of outdoor ovens, and the simple elegance and snugness that the presence of these pieces evoke in a room is unmatched. Such a fireplace could certainly be left as it is, or it could be embellished with a singular tile design that outlines the mouth of the fireplace or edges the hearth or mantel.

Above and opposite: Glass mosaic is a dream-product for creative design. Here it is used to cover a small bedside table and one wall, thus creating a stunning backdrop for the simple, understated furniture and giving this bedroom an ultra-modern touch.

BATHROOMS

Materials used for bathrooms today are similar to those used in the very first baths: green marble, purple (Phrygia) marble, soft yellows, and whites. These stones were used because they captured the warmth in the air. Marble is also extremely durable and not very porous, and is therefore an excellent choice for bathroom design. It is more resistant to staining from cosmetics and cleansers than other stones you may consider installing. Granite is also a popular choice in bathroom design because of its resilience and durability.

Ceramic tile is, of course, one of the most popular materials to be used in the bathroom. It is

Left: Combined with tumbled limestone, antique white hexagon floor tiles and rectangular tiles on the walls set the stage for a soft, romantic bathroom. *Above*: Lovely blackberry relief border designs in muted hues can add a sense of antiquity to any room.

easy to maintain and is available in a large array of colors, patterns, styles, and sizes. You may commission a large pictorial tile mural of a dreamy landscape with soothing scenes—water lilies and stone foot bridges, or a misty garden in trompe l'oeil—to set the room's theme. Another approach to creating atmosphere in the bath is to envoke an idyllic place with the design materials themselves. Achieve a

Opposite: Bathing is serene in this quiet niche, which is clad in soft, tumbled natural stone. Using the stone from floor to ceiling is the key to the success of this design. *Above:* Stunning textured concrete tiles are perfect in this contemporary lavatory.

look of Gothic romanticism with 6" by 6" (15 by 15cm) antique terra-cotta tile used in concert with a hand-cut and hand-molded decorated tile pattern in the same range of hues. The inherent romance of a French antique terra-cotta tile can not be overappreciated when it is used with a stylized art deco tile reminiscent of the technology and symbolism of its period.

Bathroom designs often incorporate tile and stone simply for their beauty. Limestone, one of the softer natural stones, is perfectly suitable for baths after an initial application of sealer. It is neutral and soothing and certainly a classic that fits almost any type of house. Tumbled limestones are also extremely comfortable and casual. Marble, honed smooth

(continued on page 131)

Above: A mosaic "rug" with a nautical theme makes this elegant bathroom more artistic and personal. The cream-colored tiles used on the floor, wall, and sink allow the mosaic design to take center stage. *Opposite:* Glossy marine-blue tiles with a simple navy border make a bold color statement in this otherwise neutral bath.

Opposite: Modernity and antiquity meet
in this exquisite bath. Relief tiles form a
border above the sink, but give way to a trompe
l'oeil painting of a Greek city. ***Above, left***:
Floor-to-ceiling luster tiles offset with light-
toned, highly textured crackle-glazed accents
create a dramatic bathroom design. ***Above***:
Softly glazed and gently pillowed tiles with
classical moldings are superb in traditional
baths and kitchens. ***Left***: Here, multicolored
tiles line the entire tub and shower area,
resulting in a playful, free-spirited bathroom.

rather than polished, is quite formal. Slates that are often available, like marble and limestone, with a matching slab for counters and baseboard are extremely easy to live with and can be found in designs from starkly modern to very casual.

Ceramic tile, however, really opens up avenues of design creativity that are unlimited. Color, size, pattern, relief art, transparency, and rustic glazes are just the tip of the iceberg. Add moldings and murals, and the wonderful variety of tile can take you from fourteenth-century England to the twenty-first century and beyond.

Left: Transparent glass tiles line the shower stall of this bathroom, which is blessed with a breathtaking ocean view. The cool, tranquil tones are conducive to a long, relaxing bath.
Above: This brilliant glass and ceramic school of fish is perfect for a home near the water.

GUEST BATHROOMS AND POWDER ROOMS

The guest bath or powder room affords you a wonderful opportunity to try designing a stone or tile mosaic for the enjoyment of your guests. A design that incorporates spiral waves, spouting fountains, marine life, and icons of the classical period used against blue and green luster or crackle-glazed tiles and field tiles may be the perfect option for this room. As these are generally small-scale rooms, more detailed and small-scale tile designs such as mosaics are ideal.

Opposite: Lovely biblical stone from Israel and antique flagstones are showcased in this austere bathroom. **Above:** Decorative tiles with deep relief patterns and simple borders can create a welcoming environment in a guest bath.

You may also experiment with ceramic tiles here, creating a random pattern of 1" by 1" (2.5 by 2.5cm) tiles installed from floor to ceiling, with the color range moving from darker tones at the floor to lighter-colored tiles near the ceiling. The optical effect of a random pattern of smaller tiles displayed in this manner becomes a dramatic backdrop for accessories and makes the room appear larger. This approach will result in a very beautiful environment that is both visually exciting and serene.

Above: A border of stone offset with glass tiles adds depth and a splash of color to this classic white "brick" tile. *Above, right*: A white running leaf border adds interest to this backsplash. *Right*: Soft, tumbled marble creates a warm contrast to this bold glass sink, in a perfect blending of traditional and contemporary styles. *Opposite*: Charming tile details for the wainscoting and mirror surround change a small, functional bath into a great one.

Opposite: Although this bathroom is pure white, the variety of relief patterns on the tiles provides plenty of visual interest. *Above*: Soft sea colors in crisp ceramic tile meet a light and clean limestone floor to create a beautiful and utilitarian bath.

A KIDS' BATH

Designing for kids is an opportunity to use all of your talents in one place: when designing a children's bathroom, the two most important factors you should consider are safety and fun.

Start by choosing a good nonslip flooring material, such as unglazed tiles to surround the tub and cover the shower area. Countertops may be tiled in a complementary color. The kids' bath is the perfect place to install the charming deco tiles, drop-ins, and borders you have fallen in love with but don't know where to use.

Placing tiles that featuring hopping bunnies or chugging tugboats around the corners of a counter serves a double function: the tiles are entertaining enough to keep kids in the bathroom long enough to get clean, and they also help make the edges and corners of counters more obvious—an important safety consideration.

If the deco tiles and border aren't providing enough entertainment, add a six- or eight-tile mural or jungle mosaic above the tub. A tile mural is a favorite among kids, for it gives them an opportunity to make up stories and games during bath time. It can also make your life a little easier, since it gives children the idea that bathing is a wonderfully exciting activity.

Opposite: These charming animal tiles are handpainted in London. *Above:* Traditional Old English alphabet tiles with a crackle glaze are perfect for a child's bath. *Below:* Handpainted tile has loads of personality and provides tons of fun for kids.

GLOSSARY

Arabesque: An intricate pattern of interlacing lines formed from flower, leaf, and occasionally animal motifs. Islamic tiles are noted for this style of decoration.

Atelier: An artist's studio.

Azulejos: From the Arabic *al zulaich*, meaning "little stone." Moroccan or Spanish tiles that are glazed and cut to form star patterns.

Ceramic: Items, including tiles and pottery, made from clay and fired in a kiln.

Classical: Anything of or relating to ancient Greece or Rome, including styles of architecture and decorative designs.

Craze: A random pattern of fine lines or cracks on the surface of a crackle-glazed tile.

Earthenware: Ceramics made of opaque, slightly porous clay that is fired at a relatively low heat.

Granite: A very hard igneous rock with a visibly crystalline, granular texture. It is a popular building material and is often used for counters and tabletops.

Greek key: A classical pattern of right-angled vertical and horizontal lines that is generally used for borders.

Guilloche: A classical motif where two or more lines are intertwined to form a shape that resembles a twisted rope, but with round openings between the intersections of the lines.

Kiln: A special oven used to dry and harden clay objects in a process called firing.

Lattice tiles: Tiles formed of crossed strips with open spaces between them, often used to decorate walls in ancient Rome because they allow light and air to come through.

Limestone: A type of sedimentary rock that is formed from an accumulation of organic remains, such as shells and coral. The colors vary greatly, from white to rose to gold, and it is a popular choice for use on floors.

Luster tiles: These tiles have an iridescent metallic sheen on the surface that allows the deeper colors of the underlying glaze to show through.

Majolica: A type of fired red earthenware that is coated with an opaque tin glaze, which is then decorated before firing. Majolica was developed in ancient Persia, but Italy became famous for its production.

Marble: The hardest of the variations of limestone. Prized for its ability to maintain a high polish, marble either can have a visibly granular texture or can be veined.

Mosaic: A pattern or picture composed of tiny pieces of stone, tile, glass, or pottery fitted together.

Pavers: Flat tile or stone blocks designed specifically for use on floors and walkways.

Pillow-cut: A type of tile with edges that are softly tapered to create a shape like a puffy pillow.

Porcelain: A hard, transparent, nonporous white clay, used for decorative tiles and fine tableware.

Quarry tile: Tile made from clay that is fired at a very high temperature to make it durable.

Relief: A figure or pattern that stands out from the surface of a tile.

Roji: The path in a Japanese garden. It is intended to make a person discontinue all thoughts of the outside world so that he or she can begin meditation.

Slate: A very fine-grained metamorphic rock that is easily split into relatively thin slabs. It is prized for its many color variations, which include blue-gray, deep charcoal, rose, and olive.

Stoneware: Ceramics made of strong, opaque, nonporous clay that is fired at a high temperature.

Terra-cotta: Hard molded and fired clay that is used for tile, floor pavers, and sculpture. The most common terra-cotta is a dark red-orange, but colors vary depending on the trace elements it contains.

Tessera: A four-cornered unit of stone, glass, tile, or marble used in mosaics.

Travertine: A hard type of limestone that can be polished to resemble marble.

Trencadis: A traditional mosaic technique from Catalan, Spain, where whole tiles are shattered into fragments, then reassembled and mortared into place.

Trompe l'oeil: From the French, meaning "to fool the eye." It is a painting technique in which objects are depicted in extremely lifelike detail with the intention of tricking the viewer into thinking the objects are real.

BIBLIOGRAPHY

Berendsen, Anne. *Tiles, A General History*. Viking Press, 1967.

Breeze, Carla. *Pueblo Deco*. Rizzoli International Publications, Inc., 1990.

Bussagli, Mario. *Oriental Architecture*. Harry S. Abrams, Inc., Publishers, 1973.

Goodwin, Elaine M. *Decorative Mosaics*. Henry Holt and Company, 1992.

Goodwin, Godfrey. *Islamic Spain*. Chronicle Books, 1990.

Hamburger, Sydney K. *Safe Spaces & Ritual Objects*. Hood College Press, 1993.

Itoh, Teiji, trans., Ralph Friedrich and Masajiro Shimamura. *Space & Illusion in the Japanese Garden*. Weatherhillt Tankosha, 1973.

Kent, Conrad, and Dennis Prindle. *Park Güell*. Princeton Architectural Press, 1993.

Kristof, Spiro. *A History of Architecture, Settings and Rituals*. Oxford University Press, 1985.

Lawler, Anthony. *The Temple in the House*. G.P. Putnam & Sons, 1994.

Lippard, Lucy R. *Overlay, Contemporary Art History and The Art of Prehistory*. The New Press, 1983.

Mann, A.T. *Sacred Architecture*. Element Books, 1993.

Okakura, Kakuzo. *The Book of Tea*. Dover Publications, Inc., 1964.

Tessa, Paul. *Tiles for a Beautiful Home*. Barron's Educational Series, 1990.

Sharkey, John. *Celtic Mysteries: The Ancient Religion*. Thames and Hudson, 1991.

Speaks, Michael, Ed. *Architecture As Metaphor*. MIT Press, 1995.

Thacker, Christopher. *A History of Gardens*. University of California Press, 1979.

Tigerman, Stanley. *The Architecture of Exile*. Rizzoli International Publications, Inc., 1988.

Watson, Walter Crum. *Portuguese Architecture*. Archibald Constable and Company, Ltd., 1908.

Yegul, Frikret. *Baths and Bathing in Classical Antiquity*. MIT Press, 1992.

Yoshikawa, Isao. *Stone Basins, The Accents of the Japanese Garden*. Graphic-sha Publishing Co. Ltd., 1989.

INDEX

PHOTO CREDITS

©Ken Anderson & Miriam Seeger: p. 44 (designer: Brian Rudd, Smith Custom Estates)

Courtesy of Anima Ceramics: p. 42 top (designer: Lucinda Johnson of Anima Ceramic Design); p. 131 right (designer: Lucinda Johnson of Anima Ceramic Design)

Courtesy of Ann Sacks Tile & Stone: pp. 90, 117

©Michael Arden: pp. 40-41 (designers: Balaban & Shapiro and Hub of the House)

Art Resource, NY: ©Erich Lessing: pp. 14, 25, 73; ©Scala: p. 13 top, 26; ©Werner Forman Archive: p. 29 left

©Tim Benko; Tiles by Fire & Earth Ceramics: pp. 36 left; p. 20 (designer: Karen Marx)

©Laurie Black: pp. 47, 102 (designer: Ann Sacks)

©Frederick Charles: pp. 17, 99 (Bogdanow Partners Architects, NY)

©David Clifton: p. 126 (designers: Pappageorge/Haymes, Ltd.)

©Grey Crawford: p. 63 (designer: Bebe Winkler Interior Design)

©Phillip Ennis: pp. 89, 91 (designer: Nicholas Caulder & Associates)

Courtesy of Fire & Earth Ceramics: p. 129 top left (designer: Connie Hill)

©Nick Garribo: p. 4-5, 104 (designer: Rhonda Knoche of Neil Kelly Designers/ Remodelers)

©Jamie Hadley: p. 123 (designer: Michael Agins)

©Jerome Hart: p. 105 (designer: Dana Louis)

©Alec Hemer: pp. 118, 119 (designer: Catherine Gerry of Catherine Gerry Interiors)

©David Inbal: pp. 72 top, 132 (designer: David Inbal)

©Jon Jensen; Courtesy of *Traditional Home*: pp. 74, 120-121 left, 134 top right

©Elliot Kaufman: p. 36 right-37 (designer: Kutnicki Bernstein Associates)

Courtesy of Kohler Co.: pp. 23 left, 46 top left, 80, 122, 125, 128, 134 bottom right; p. 66 (designer: Todd Graf of Ann Sacks Tile & Stone, Kohler, WI); pp. 30, 31 (designer: Cynthia Retzlaff); p. 34 (designer: Vic Samaritoni of Ann Sacks Tile & Stone, Kohler, WI)

©Don Leddick: pp. 6-7, 38 (designer: Beverly Hammel of Rutt of Chicago)

©Peter Ledwith: p. 83, 136 (designer: Marci Feigen of Ann Sacks Tile & Stone, NY)

Leo de Wys, Inc.: ©Jon Hicks: p. 13 bottom, 49 left, 70 right; © Jean Paul Nacivet: p. 15; ©Steve Vidler: pp. 10 right, 28 bottom, 48, 50

©David Livingston: p. 115; p. 112 (designer: Lou Ann Bauer); pp. 100 (designer: Kuleto); 127 (designer: Nancy Scheinholtz)

©Peter Malinowski/InSite: p. 88 (designer: Agnes Bourne, Inc. and Geoffrey DeSousa)

©Dave Marlow; Tiles by Fire & Earth Ceramics: p. 124

Courtesy of Meredith Corporation: pp. 58-59 left, 71 (designer: Doug Rasar, Seattle)

©William Nettles: p. 114 (designer: Carol Beth Cozen); p. 113 (designer: Sheri Hirschfeld)

©Mary E. Nichols: p. 95, 108, 109, 137 (designer: Joe Ruggiero & Associates)

©Gary Parker: p. 135 (designers: Miller/Stein)

©Undine Prohl: pp. 130-131 left (designer: Ron Goldman)

©Kenneth Rice: p. 54 (designer: Ginny Kelsey)

©Evan Richman: pp. 65, 79 (designer: Janet Feher of Ann Sacks Tile & Stone, NY & William Costine of Allan Greenberg Architects, NY)

©Jonathan Safir: p. 43 both (designers: Zoo Gang Studios)

©Jeremy Samuelson: p. 22 (architect: James Harlan, Los Angeles)

©Miriam Seger: pp. 32 all, 33 all, 35 both, 39 bottom row, 41 right columns, 42 bottom rows, 44 bottom row, 46 right column and bottom row, 59 left both, 60 all, 64 all, 67 all, 70 left, 72 bottom row, 76 bottom right, 96 all, 121 right, 139 all

©Beth Singer: p. 116 (designer: Ann Sacks)

©Holly Stickley: pp. 110-111 both (designer: Linda Bradshaw Allen); p. 133 (designers: Erin Connell & George Tsaconas); pp. 16, 56 (European Bath, Kitchen Tile & Stone, Las Vegas, NV); pp. 2 (room designer: Janet Edwards of Sandra Lamer Interiors; floor designer: Dennis Clemens, Architect), 82, 138 (designer: Janet Edwards of Sandra Lamer Interiors); pp. 19, 85, 92, 97, 129 bottom (designer: William Hefner); p. 84, 129 top right (designer: Melody Hendry of European Bath, Kitchen, Tile & Stone with Danielle Polvorosa of Ann Sacks Tile & Stone, Portland, OR); p. 18 (designer: Neil Kelly, Portland, OR; paint specs by Art First, Portland, OR); p. 55, 62, 81 (designer: Sandra Lamer of Sandra Lamer Interiors); p. 45 (designer: Sandra Lindsay); p. 140 (designers: Marks & Marks Design); p. 61 (designer: RCI, Inc. & George Capistani of Caracol); p. 78, 103, 107 (designer: Barbara Schnitzler); p. 101 (designer: Linda Scott of Scott Design & Associates); p. 134 left (designers: Stuart Silk with *Country Living* Magazine—*Country Living*'s 1998 House of the Year); p. 21 (designer: Dirk Stennick); p. 23 right (designer: Holly Stickley with Ann Sacks

©Roger Turk: p. 77 (designer: Leslie Galvin)

©Peter Vitale: p. 86 (designer: Sandi Van Vliet and Steve Chase of Steve Chase Associates)

©Paul Wear: p. 93 (tiles by Fire & Earth Ceramics)

Woodfin Camp & Associates: ©John Blaustein: p. 10 left; ©Winston Conrad: pp. 51, 52; ©Robert Frerck: pp. 11, 27, 28 top, 29 right, 49 right, 53; ©R & S Michaud: p. 12 left; ©Adam Woolfitt: pp. 8, 12 right; ©Mike Yamashita: p. 9

©Mark Woods: pp. 57, 76 top row and bottom left, 68 all, 69 all; p. 39 top (artist & designer: Rebecca Gore); pp. 94, 106 (designer: Cynthia Stroum); endpapers